50/Fifty

Sowmya Moni

Illustrations by the author

BookLeaf Publishing

India | USA | UK

Presentation by *BookLeaf Publishing*

Web: www.bookleafpub.com

E-mail: info@bookleafpub.com

ISBN: 9789363312609

First edition 2024

ACKNOWLEDGEMENT

This book wouldn't exist without my friends and colleagues. Thank you for the shared laughter, whispered frustrations, and inspiring resilience that fueled these poems.

PREFACE

At fifty, life demands a new epic poem—and who is better to craft it than a woman navigating the battleground of corporate India? These poems don't shy away from the battlefield; they embrace it.

Within these pages, you will find the quiet strength of Sita in a deal negotiation, the strategic brilliance of Durga in the corporate boardroom, and yes, even a touch of Kali's righteous fury when facing workplace injustice.

CONTENTS

Durga Rising

Durga, in Sanskrit दुर्गा, *means 'invincible'.*

"So, you are turning **50** in a few months," a
female colleague asked,
"I bet you have embraced menopause and the
bone loss to follow,
But, amidst the time you have left, what's the
joy you wish to borrow?"
Well, it's not a hot flash but a power surge like
Kali, so there!
Watching Shark Tank India recently brought
reprieve that there are even color
extensions for lost hair.
At 50, she's like a butterfly in the rain,
She's waiting for the sunshine to spread her
wings again.

She's weathered many storms and faced her share of pain,
But she's ready for the next chapter, and she's not the one to complain.
Embracing this new chapter with fire and fun,
Because life at **Fifty** has only just begun!

Instant Lakshmi

***Lakshmi**, in Sanskrit लक्ष्मी, is derived from the root words lakṣ (लक्ष्) and lakṣa (लक्ष), meaning 'to know' and 'goal', respectively. These root words give Lakshmi the symbolism: to know your goal.*

In today's multi-generational teams, we see Gen [X, Y, Z]'s relationship with Lakshmi is different and unique.
Gen X seeks a stable career,
With a house and an SUV, they hold dear.
Their Lakshmi goal is financial security,
And to live a life of comfort and stability.

Gen Y, the millennials, seek fame and followers galore,
Their Lakshmi goal is 'Insta' likes and more!
With 100, 50, 20, and 10 hacks to moneyball,
They seem to work smart and think they understand it all.
Gen Z, the zoomers, are entrepreneurs at heart,
With many side hustles that are waiting to kick-start.
Guap is money, a.k.a. Lakshmi, and lots of it, they desire,
They hustle and grind if Gen X and Gen Y inspire.

Saraswati – The AI Agent

***Saraswati**, in Sanskrit सरस्वती, means 'the one who possesses eloquence in speech and has high intellect'.*

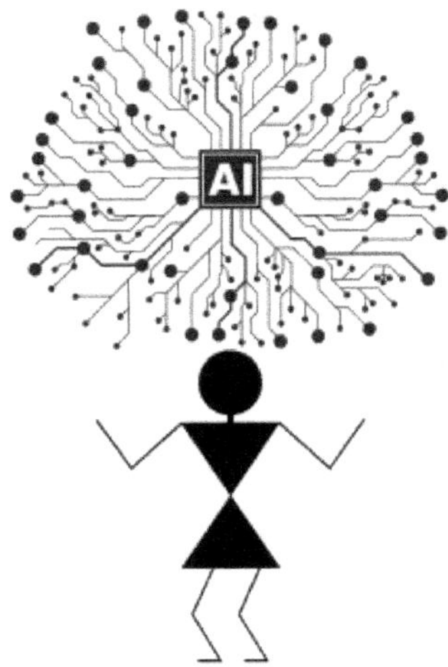

Saraswati is their AI agent of automation,
Powering mundane tasks and workflows with
GPT innovation.
She'll spin you a poem that's sure to bring cheer,
Or answer your questions, making everything
clear.

With tokens and prompts, Saraswati's mind
flows,
A friend for all feelings as AI grows.
They pray to her every day at the office,
Dear Saraswati, they seek your wisdom so dear.
But when the answer reveals what they fear,
They'll turn a blind eye and pretend it's not there.
And hope for better insights next time, if they
care!

Shailaputri Moonshots

Shailaputri *means the daughter (putri) of mountain (shaila). She symbolizes woman power.*

Shailaputris in the corporate world show
courage to make their mark,
They bet on moonshots to light a spark.
"We've got the solution," they proudly claim,
As if it's groundbreaking, but it's all the same.
Customers nod along, playing their part,
Humoring the company with a beat in their
heart.
Design thinking is what they call this latest
trend,
But sometimes it feels like it is the same means
to an end.

Customer says, "Isn't this what I already do?"
but Shailaputris are bold, they know the
game,
They'll sell you the moon and make you think
it's not the same.
Raise a glass to these trailblazers, if you dare,
Cheers to them for taking risks with flair.

Rama and Lakshmana Ki Jodi

***Rama**, in Sanskrit राम, is the main protagonist, and **Lakshmana**, in Sanskrit लक्ष्मण, is the younger brother of Rama in the mythological epic Ramayana.*

My manager tells me, as a newbie in this place,
Meet my Anmol "Ratans," Rama and
Lakshmana dear,
Like Kohinoor jewels, they're revered year after
year.
He says, "They're the extraordinary league,
With skills so sharp, they're truly unique.
For they hold the company's fate in their hands,
But don't worry, they'll help you stand."
Why do they presume, frogs in the well, know it
all,
When really, they just have a small pond so tall!

Clean Ganga in Copper Bottle

Ganga, *in Sanskrit* गङ्गा, *means 'swift goer' and is associated with purity, fertility, and new beginnings.*

Drink water from copper bottles, they say,
Stay away from 'whites' in flour and sugar,
every day.
They say our wellness is their goal,
Copper has minerals like distilled Ganga for
purifying the body and soul.
Perhaps, it's time to rethink about spamming
inboxes with emails without care,
And stop adding to the digital pollution we
already share.
Let's be mindful of the emails and meeting
invites we send,
And work towards a cleaner and greener digital
trend.

Karma Theory

Karma, in Sanskrit कर्म, refers to an action, work, or deed and its effect or consequences.

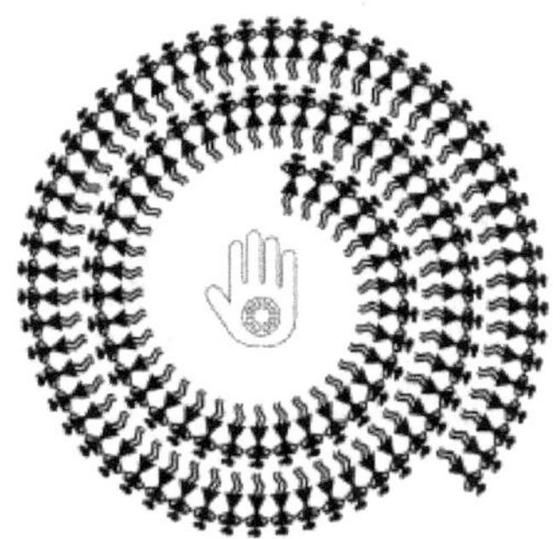

The theory of Karma, you see,
Says every event is the outcome of a past deed.
A players, B players, all have roles,
They fight and debate for single-digit pay hikes
and dry promotion at play,
They know their fate before they start the year.
But deliver performance they must, with all their
might,
And hope that good karma will make everything
right!

Narada: Growth Advisors

***Narada**, in Sanskrit नारद, is a sage famous in mythology who is a traveling musician and storyteller with enlightening wisdom.*

In the world of early, mid, late stage start-ups,
there's a curious breed,
They go by as growth advisors with wisdom and
unseen power indeed.
They challenge assumptions and stir up emotion,
Leaving employees in a whirlwind of
commotion.
They're paid hefty sums for their wisdom and
insight,
Providing fodder to steer the ship just right.
Like the lute-wielding sage, Narada, "Narayana,
Narayana," they may chant and sing,
Watching the daily office dramas from afar and
their impact is a whole other thing!

Kali on Corporate Boards

Kali, in Sanskrit काली, is associated with change, creation, and power.

Indian corporate boards are in a bind,
They need more women with the power of mind,
A Kali they seek, fierce and bold,
To bring truth to light, and secrets unfold.
But Kali doesn't care about being nice,
She'll call out the hidden truths without thinking twice.
The boards fear her fiery gaze,
For she sees through their financial maze.
So bring on the Kali, with her no-nonsense ways,
She'll shake up the boardroom for better days.
With her strength and wisdom, she'll set things right,
And corporate governance will see the light!

Sanjaya's Polaroid

***Sanjaya**, in Sanskrit* सञ्जय, *means 'victory'. He was the advisor of the blind king Dhritarashtra in the mythological epic Mahabharata.*

Chiefs of Staff are Sanjayas with the gift of
divine vision,
For C-suite, who is often blind to the chaos, they
guide the way.
Like a Polaroid picture, they capture it all,
With opinions as frank as a wake-up call.
They share every incident of the daily
Kurukshetra, from operations to sales, from
employees at war with managers, with grace,
Guiding their leaders through every challenge
they face.

Devi Diversity

Devi, *in Sanskrit* देवी, *means 'the highest form of excellence'.*

On Women's Day, men celebrate with pink,
But now, they are encouraging women to also
pause and think,
They are celebrating women like Devis they
adore,
But do they not know, equality in pay and work
is what women are really looking for.
Vouchers, gifts, special lunches, panel talks on
empowerment sound grand,
But actions speak louder when the real need is to
take a stand.
Devis on Women's Day, make it clear,
They want real change, not just once a year.

Rama in Exile

Rama, in Sanskrit राम, is the male protagonist of
the Ramayana. Rama's life is described in the
Hindu texts as one challenged by unexpected
changes, such as a forest exile for 14 years.

Tenured employees are like Rama in forest exile,
they say,
Should be rewarded for their humility and
loyalty each day.
They are like banyan trees, offering generous
shade but hindering the budding of new
grass,
They're timeless and venerable, still struggling
for a fresh start.
Will they readily welcome a woman leader for a
change?

Or adhere to the past, steadfastly within their
range?
Their experience is valuable, that much is true,
But they need to sprout some new shoots too!

Yashoda Instinct

Yashoda, in Sanskrit यशोदा, *means one who is a giver (da,* दा*) of fame or glory (Yash,* यश*).*

They celebrate wins, big and small,
And lift their team when they stumble and fall.
For it's not just profits they strive to gain,
But growth and well-being that truly sustain.
They foster a culture of trust and care,
Where every team member feels valued and
rare.
She'll fight for your raise, with the fury of ten,
If you're lucky enough to have Yashoda in your
den.
Here's to the leaders, with hearts so wide,
Who embodies compassion with every stride.
The Yashoda Instinct is a gift so grand,
Transforming great places to work across the
land.

Gandhari Vision

Gandhari *is a prominent figure in the*
Mahabharata, who is depicted with a blindfold,
which she wore to live like her blind husband.

A blindfold bound, as a sign of silent protest, is
a choice she made,
Transcending physical limitations and inner
fortitude she displayed.
Blindfolded she was, but not in her mind,
Her wisdom and insight were one of a kind.
Though darkness veiled her eyes from view,
Her spirit shone, her strength rang true.
Corporate Gandharis, not every battle needs to
be seen,

Strength often lies in actions, quiet and keen.
Like her wisdom, let your insight take hold,
True power whispers for great stories to be told.

Vasudhaiva Kutumbakam

"Vasudhaiva Kutumbakam," the CEO proclaims
at the beginning of every year with glee,
"We're a family here!" he declares, "Just like
IPL, you see!"
We nod and smile politely but behind our forced
grins,
We know the truth, dear colleagues, how this
corporate saga spins.
We're drafted for our talents rare, like batsmen
brave and true,

Data wizards, code conjurers, with stories fresh
and new.
Like fielders poised for catches, we're ready for
each task,
On and off the field, in victory and fame, we
may bask.
But when the fiscal innings end and balance
sheets turn red,
The corporate pitch goes south, filled with doubt
and dread.
The 'family' warmth evaporates, replaced by icy
fear,
As whispers of 'restructuring' echo in our ears.
Suddenly, we're not Kohli, Sharma, hitting sixes
in the sun,
We're unsold players, benched and glum, our
corporate innings done.
The pink slips flutter down, like confetti tinged
with dread,
"We appreciate your service," the HR manager
said.
"But market forces, you know how they play,"
And just like that, our 'family' sends us on our
way.

Agni Pariksha

***Agni Pariksha**, in Sanskrit अग्निप्रवेशम्, means 'trial by fire', which is primarily associated with the ordeal of Sita in the Ramayana.*

The corporate Sitas face the test,
Like Agni Pariksha, they must impress,
To rise above and claim their seat,
In the boardroom, where the powerfuls meet and greet.
Like Sita, they must face the flames with grace,
Proving their worth in this competitive space.
They don't want quotas on corporate boards,
But climbing the ladder is no easy accord.
For when they pass the test, we all gain,
Closer to equality, breaking the male-only chain.

Garudas in Flight

Garuda, in Sanskrit गरुड, *is described as the king of the birds and a symbol of speed and martial prowess.*

Garuda came with fire, a fledgling fresh and
bold,
To learn and grow, crafting new corporate stories
to be told.
"An internship's the way," the mentors all had
cried,
"Prove your worth," they said, "And you'll soar
the ride!"
"Fetch this report," the marketing leader cries,
"Analyze that data," the finance head replies.
"Optimize this process," the operations chief
commands,
Garuda spins and spins, caught in their demands.

From team to team he's tossed, a pawn in their
game,
Each manager's whim, a wildfire, burning the
same.
His spirit wanes, the fire flickers low,
Is this the fate for a Garuda to know?
A cog in the machine, dreams starting to rust,
Will he break free or crumble into dust?
For Garuda's spirit cannot be contained,
By cubicles and deadlines, his purpose
unchained.
He'll learn and grow; on his own terms, he'll fly,
A Garuda's journey, reaching for the sky.

Draupadi Shield

Draupadi, in Sanskrit द्रौपदी, *was the main female protagonist of the Mahabharata. She was known for her beauty and courage.*

The glass ceiling gleams, a deceptive sheen,
Where whispers wound and doubts cut sharp and keen.
But Draupadi's gaze holds unwavering might,
For Krishna's counsel is her guiding light.
"When deals seem lost," he whispers, calm and low,
"Remember Dharma, let integrity grow.
For every Duryodhana, with his cunning ploy,
There's strength within you to counter and destroy."
The boardroom trembles, with each strategic stride,
As Draupadi speaks, her voice is both clear and wide.
Her words are arrows, piercing through the haze,

Of ego, greed, and corporate's murky ways.
"This isn't just a game," her message rings out true,
"We build, we innovate, with purpose in view.
Our people, our planet, deserve far more than gain,
A better future, where compassion will reign."

Cost-Performance Ratio

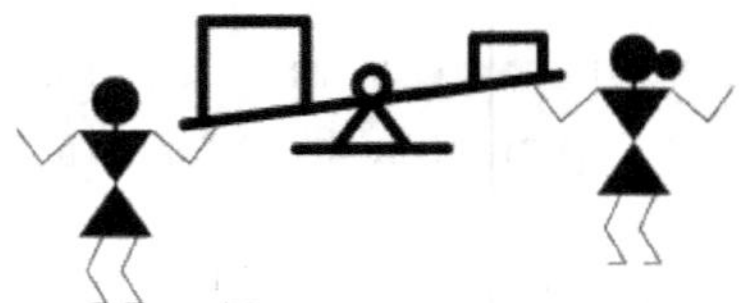

In the land of Bharat, where myths unfold,
A tale of labor and worth, ages old.
Like Lakshmi's coins, unevenly bestowed,
On men and women, though equal loads they've
towed.
Durga's strength, in boardrooms rarely prized,
Her skills, like Saraswati, are often
unrecognized.
For every rupee that Rama might earn,
Sita's hands, though equally skilled, there is less
in return.
In today's corporate world, this tale persists,
A woman's worth, in pay, is still missed.
Her efforts, while silent and profound,
Are often met with shadows, whispers, and
seldom crowned.
Her performance, even though is stellar and her
dedication is clear,
Yet her earnings lag, year after year.

Finding Hanuman

Hanuman, in Sanskrit हनुमान्, *is revered as a
divine 'vanara' and a devoted companion of
Rama in the Ramayana.*

In the corporate world, CEOs relentlessly roam,
Searching for their own Hanuman to bring them
home,
Like in the Ramayana, they seek a magical cure,
To salvage dead projects and make their profits
sure.
They search for heroes to save the day,
Like Hanuman finding Sanjeevani on his way,
With escalating customers and overruns, making
them stay,
To keep the company from going astray.
So, if you're ready to be the Hanuman in the
corporate sea,

Get ready to swing from project to project, like a
monkey,
Remember, in the corporate enterprise,
You can be the magical herb that money can't
buy!

Vaikuntha – The Promised Land

Vaikuntha, in Sanskrit वैकुण्ठ, *means 'heaven'.*

In the land of startups, there lies a dream, a
promised land,
Vaikuntha, they call it, shining bright,
Where ESOPs may turn to gold overnight.
Finding the holy grail, as some would call
product-market fit, that's the key,
To unlock the gates of prosperity.
They pivot and iterate, tweak and refine,
Until their offering is close to divine.
They toil and hustle, day and night,
Coding and pitching with all their might.
In corporate boardrooms and cafes, they plot and
plan,
Hoping for that golden IPO to land.
The CEO chants, "Hold on tight,
Vaikuntha is near; it's within sight."

But the journey's long and the path unclear,
Employees hold their breath with tingling fear.
Their shares, they dangle like a carrot on a stick,
The lure of financial independence and early
retirement—should they call it a trick?
They pray to the Gods of the market floor,
"Please let the stock price soar and soar!"
So, here's to the dreamers, the ESOP holders,
and the startup crew,
May Vaikuntha's doors open for you and your
IPO, too.

Detachment Lesson from Gita

*The **Bhagavad Gita**, in Sanskrit भगवद्गीता, is a 700-verse Hindu scripture that is a part of the Mahabharata.*

In the corporate world, succession planning is key,
Just like in the Bhagavad Gita, it's about detachment, you see.
Detach from the outcome, give it your best shot,
And let go of the past glory if it's all you've got.
Train your successor with love and care,
Share your knowledge, elevate your game, and be fair.
Let go of control with a smile,
And watch your legacy grow, mile by mile.

Corporate Devas and Asuras

Deva, *in Sanskrit* देव, *means 'anything of excellence', and* **Asura**, *in Sanskrit* असुर, *means 'power seeking'.*

At corporates today, we see asuras lead with
insecurity and fear,
They steal your limelight, and their
power-hungry ways are crystal clear.
They thrive on control and rule with an iron
hand,
But their leadership skills are not in high
demand.
On the other hand, the devas lead with grace,
Inspiring others with a smile on their face.
They value teamwork and foster a positive vibe,

Their leadership style is one that we all should imbibe.
When joining a company or a team, do your due diligence,
Managing a deva or asura leader or manager will test your patience and tolerance.

Indra's War and Peace

Indra, in Sanskrit इन्द्र, is the king of the devas in Hinduism, who is associated with the sky, lightning, weather, thunder, storms, rains, river flows, and war.

Climate change is slowly and surely affecting us all,
Overflowing rivers, melting glaciers, hotter summers, and colder winters—is it Indra at war?
On Earth Day and during customer visits, saplings are gifted with care,
Seems just a tiny band-aid on the environmental wear and tear,
Sowing the seeds for the future is their noble goal,

But sometimes, it feels like they're cleverly
managing a CSR loophole.
Employees are told to take the pledge of
greening the planet on Earth Day,
But what about the other 364, do they throw
their pledges away?
It's great to see them trying to make a change,
Or is it tokenism to uplift the corporate image?
There are valiant 'Greenpeace' warriors pushing
for real change, that's for sure,
Searching for safer fuels and bringing order back
to nature is the cure!

Remembering Gita in Chai Conversations

*Chapter 17, verse 15 of the **Bhagavad Gita** says that people should speak words that are truthful, pleasant, beneficial, and not agitate anyone.*

In our corporates, every day feels like judgment day,
Validation from customers, peers, managers, and leaders, you deeply care what they say,
Watercooler or Chai conversations are seemingly benign,
But is it you or your credibility, folks at work wish to malign?

As they waste time with idle conversation,
You're achieving goals, gaining admiration.
Living rent-free in their minds, even if they were
once your mate.
They may say no malice in intent, so no harm is
done,
Just sharing the news, having a little fun.
So, next time you hear a juicy office tale,
Remember the Gita, and let the truth prevail!

Krishna – The Visionary Leader

Krishna, in Sanskrit कृष्ण, is a major deity in Hinduism, who is considered the God of protection, compassion, tenderness, and love.

In Kurukshetra, Krishna led the way,
With visionary leadership, he saved the day.
He chose Arjuna, the archer who had no peers,
And Bhima, the strongest of the brothers, to conquer everyone's fears.
Nakula and Sahadeva were also twins of might,

While wise Yudhishthira led with intellect and
insight.
Unity of purpose was their common goal,
The Pandavas, who were five, each played to
their strengths in the assigned role.
From mythical wars to today's corporate race,
Krishna's wisdom and leadership still have their
rightful place.
Krishna in his Gita lessons, so timeless and true,
Continues to guide corporate leaders in the work
they do.
He was wise and knew talent that had the
winning view,
Even today, we seek Krishna's vision in CEOs
and their leadership crew.

Ekalavya – The Self-Taught Intern

Ekalavya, in Sanskrit एकलव्य, is a character from the Mahabharata. As a youth, Ekalavya admired Drona for teaching archery to Kauravas and Pandavas. He desired to learn it from Drona, who refused, citing Ekalavya's lower caste. Undeterred, Ekalavya self-mastered archery and gave his thumb as Guru Dakshina to Drona.

Behold the interns, bright-eyed and keen,
The modern Ekalavyas, the coding human machine.
They've taught themselves Python, Node.js, and React.
They learn on the job with every project, leaving Drona wondering how their ambition is still intact?

Drona's several pressure tests they must face,
But do they know, to climb the corporate ladder,
there's a thumb to erase?
The corporate Pandavas may hold the reins for a
while,
But with the skills they've gained, Eklavyas are
ready to build a unicorn with style!

Artha in Work and Life

Artha, in Sanskrit अर्थ, means 'purpose'.

From Maslow's hierarchy of needs we learn,
At fifty and beyond, that self-actualization is
what we all ultimately yearn.
No longer just a means to a paycheck at month
end,
But a life of meaning, where love and joy
transcend.
Maslow's pyramid crumbles, as we can finally
see,
Purpose isn't linear; it's in all we do and be.
Artha is striking a balance between work and
life threads that run through,
From basic needs to the highest deeds, purpose
is actually seeking you.

Corporate Gurukulam

Gurukulam, in Sanskrit गुरुकुल, is a type of education system in ancient India with disciples living near or with the Guru in the same house for a period where they learn and get educated by their Guru.

We'll teach you skills you've never heard of before.
"Synergistic paradigm shifts," Gurus boldly proclaim,
While CEOs nod when they can't explain the learning aim.
Millions are spent on corporate training,
But returns are limited with this Gurukulam-type schooling.
Gurukulam of the old was indeed a sacred place,

Where holistic knowledge flowed with elegance
and grace.
Instead of endless PowerPoint slides,
They bestowed wisdom that truly guides,
Interactive learning with real-life experiences
just like in the Gurukulam of the old,
Where knowledge and wisdom from Gurus were
worth their weight in gold.
Now, it seems more about showing off LinkedIn
badges as success,
And the true essence of actionable learning
seems to be under duress.

Sudama Gifting

*Sudama, in Sanskrit सुदामा, means 'benefactor'.
He was a childhood friend of the Hindu deity
Krishna in the Bhagavata Purana.*

In the Bhagavata Purana, a handful of rice,
Was all poor Sudama could afford to entice,
When met his childhood friend, the mighty and
rich Krishna,
His gift was small yet filled with a lot of
bhakti-rasa.
Krishna repaid Sudama with riches manyfold,
It is a beautiful friendship tale from the days of
old.
In today's corporate world, eco-gifting is the
rage,

From seed pencils to rice pens, they are turning
a new page.
Sudama's gift was filled with love and emotion,
Shows that big wins can indeed come from
heartfelt devotion.
Corporates are perhaps taking a cue or two from
this ancient inspiration,
Rewarding dedicated employees and customers
with eco-gifting innovation.

Core Values

Core Values, in Sanskrit गुणाः, *are essential beliefs and principles that lead an individual to act or a company to operate in a certain way.*

For in the pages of mythology, we find wisdom
that still holds true,
Core values that guide us in all that we do.
With integrity like Rama, fair and just,
And teamwork like the Pandavas, in whom we
can place our trust.
Like Sita following her dharma with sincerity,
Despite questions raised about her credibility.
We can find the essence of excellence,
Like Arjuna's aim and Krishna's common sense.
We seek partnerships, like Hanuman to Rama
with his pure devotion,

Loyal and strong—a potent and winning
combination.
But beware of the cunning crooks like Shakuni,
What was once loaded dice are now books
fudged guilt-free,
Leaders in Enron and Satyam are corporate
Kauravas in bold,
Their dharma is lost for greed and sovereign
bonds of gold.
Investors like Abhimanyus are sadly caught
playing their part,
Trapped in Chakravyuha of financially
engineered art.
While regulators are slow as Bhishma's fall,
Take years to act, if they act at all.
Let's remember, core values shape the culture
and define success,
In corporate boardrooms and beyond, in work
and life, no less.

Karna – The CSR Volunteer of the Year

Karna, in Sanskrit कर्ण, means 'the ear'. He is one of the main protagonists of the Mahabharata. His generosity and his loyalty towards his friend Duryodhana compel him to sacrifice his own life on the battlefield.

In the corporate Kurukshetra of modern times,
Karna fights not with arrows but with
volunteering paradigms.
Sustainability reports are his mighty bow,
Shooting down waste and carbon footprints low.
He's the champion of causes, working day and
night,
With a heart as golden as his mythical armor
bright.

His cubicle is a shrine to every good deed done,
Plaques and trophies shine like Surya, the sun.
'Employee of the Year' barely scratches the
surface,
Karna's kindness is a shining example of selfless
service.
May we all learn from this hero's heart,
With corporate giving, let each one of us play
our part.
For in the end, it's not just profits that make us
whole,
But the Karna-like kindness that enriches the
soul.

Hastinapur – Corporate Valuation

In the Mahabharata, Hastinapur is portrayed as the capital of the Kaurava's Kuru Kingdom.

In corporate boardrooms, where profits reign supreme,
Valuing modern Hastinapur is every leader's dream.
The throne of power, not gold but in stock,
Where CEOs change and fortunes rock.
Trials and tribulations, a quarterly test,
Stakeholders watching, for who is the CEO's successor at best?
Earnings calls—the modern swayamvara,
Suitors line up, near and far.
Like Draupadi at stake, company may get divided,

Shareholders left confused and misguided.
The Dharma of good governance, for those who
rule with wisdom true,
May save a legacy, not just business value
accrued.
Hastinapur throne's true worth isn't in the
zeroes,
But in creating tomorrow's corporate ethical
heroes.

Fundraising Swayamvara

***Svayamvara**, in Sanskrit स्वयंवर, means self-choice. It is a distinctive matrimonial tradition in ancient Indian society, where the bride actively participates in selecting her husband from a gathering of eligible bachelors.*

VCs, PEs, Shark Tanks set the stage,
Where pitches fly and valuations rage.
Founders are wary, for their equity is at stake,
Which shark will bite, which deal will they make?
The Swayamvara continues, round after round,
Series A, B, C—alphabets increase abound.
Each letter a test, each test a trial,
As founders dilute, hoping for that magic dial.
Angel investors flutter with heavenly cash,
Seed rounds sprout dreams of an exit splash.

But beware the fine print, founder, and
co-founder,
For strings attached might pull you under.
The investment circle is like Kaurava princes in
bold,
Each wanting a piece of the startup gold.
"What's your TAM?" they ask as they are
questioning your integrity,
"Your CAC, your churn, do you know your path
to profitability?"
From accelerators to incubators, the journey
winds,
With each milestone reached, more equity
unwinds.
The cap table, once simple, now a complex art,
As founders balance control with a heavy heart.
That stellar listing is the ultimate Swayamvara
prize,
When private goes public, valuations do rise.
They are eager to ring the bell and pop the
bubbly so fine,
But they must remember when they borrow to
grow, there will be pressure to toe the
line.

Ganesha for Growth & Good Luck

Ganesha, *in Sanskrit गणेश, is one of the most worshiped deities in the Hindu religion. Although Ganesha has many attributes, he is readily identified by his elephant head and four arms. He is widely revered, more specifically, as the remover of obstacles and harbinger of good luck.*

In every new venture, every merger and deal,
They chant his name; it's their lucky seal.
"Ganpati Bappa Morya!" echoes through Dalal Street,
As bulls and bears dance to his divine beat.

Leaders look for Ganeshas with four arms who
can multitask with ease,
To juggle multiple projects and demanding
clients to please.
From seed funding to unicorn status, they grow,
With Ganesha's blessings, their steady funds
flow.
Revenue, EBITA, PAT can all be on a steep
incline,
If, with hard work, Ganesha in good luck
chooses to shine.

Gauri's Resilience

Gauri, in Sanskrit गौरी, *means 'brilliant'. She is the Hindu Goddess of power, energy, harmony, and motherhood.*

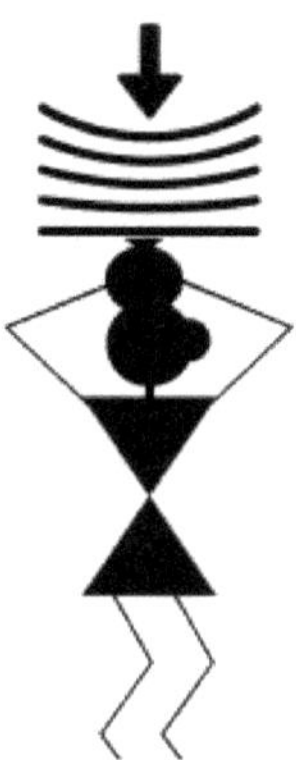

Gauri paused her career, a choice she made,
Raising kids, running the home, her priorities carefully weighed.
Mothers and caregivers, seasoned and wise,
Working from home and noticed with a fresh pair of eyes.
The gap in résumé is no longer a flaw,
As Gauri makes up for a wealth of life experience, rich and raw.
She is economy's Shakti and talented workforce,
Willing to reskill and upskill to chart her new course.

Corporate India, you're finally waking,
To the sound of the glass ceiling breaking!
In boardrooms and startups, let her influence
grow,
Gauri's resilience is certainly beginning to
show!

Yama and Taxes

Yama, in Sanskrit यम, *means 'twin'. He is the Hindu God of death and justice.*

In work and life, death and taxes, the duo, we can't shake,
A certainty that can equalize give and take.
They toil hard all month to see pockets grow light,
To pay the living tax, day and night.
They aim to save, but end up in the red,
Paying to live until they're good and near dead.
Then Yama comes, with one last tax to pay,
The final breath, the ultimate payday.
So, here's a thought, as wild as it may be,

What if we earned less, paid less, lived more
disease free?
Dodge Yama's dance and the taxman's claw,
And find some peace in this cosmic law.

Sudarshana Chakra

Sudarshana, is derived from two Sanskrit words – Su (सु) meaning 'auspicious' and Darshana (दर्शन) meaning 'vision'. The word Chakra is derived from the root क्रम् (kram) or ऋत् (rt) or क्रि (kri) and metaphorically to the wheel of time.

With strategic customers, the stakes are high,
They need a leader with a special eye.
To spot the threats and opportunities,
And spin strengths into success with deft expertise.
They need a Sudarshana Chakra to slice inefficiencies with razor edge,
Cut inflated costs and trim the bloated budget hedge.
Juggling project overruns and resourcing problems with finesse,

Turning chaos into leadership success.
Balancing the needs upon their finger,
Showing customers that they have a leader who
is a forward thinker.
For it is time for the leader to demonstrate,
Using Sudarshana Chakra can make their
leadership great.

Chanakya Niti

***Chanakya** was an ancient Indian polymath who was an author, strategist, philosopher, economist, jurist, and politician. He served as the chief advisor and prime minister of both emperors Chandragupta Maurya and his son Bindusara. Niti means 'strategy'.*

Chanakya's Arthashastra, a timeless guide,
In corporate strategy, his sutras still reside.
From Pataliputra to Wall Street's might,
Chanakya's wisdom has shown many the light.
SWOT or PEST analysis? He knew it well,
When helping Chandragupta and Bindusara excel.
From Bindusara to Bezos, the game continues to be the same,
Strategic thinking is the path to glory and fame.

Centuries ago, he helped build an empire from
the ground,
Now, his work offers counsel to the world
around.
From Mauryan courts to Silicon Valley,
His strategy continues to traverse every
corporate alley.
So, when executives feel lost at sea,
They can turn to Chanakya Niti, a.k.a. strategy.

Rama-like Capacity and Capability

In India's tech parks, which have hi-rise glass
buildings gleaming and vast,
Where coders rule and deadlines move fast,
In cubicle farms, row after row,
We see this conundrum that clearly shows,
"We've got the headcount!" the managers beam,
But client-ready skills and capability are still but
a dream.
Capacity they boast in numbers grand,
But billable hours? Not yet on hand.
Capacity is the volume they hold,
The number of tasks that can unfold,
But capability is a different beast,

It's skill and talent, to say the least.
So, when they staff the next big project,
They should not let this difference go
unchecked.
Ten Ravanas might fill the floor,
But one skilled Rama can give them more.
Like Rama's small army, skilled and true,
That overcame Lanka's larger crew.
Leaders like Rama must know the difference,
though fewer in sum,
A capable team can outperform the unskilled
one.

Brahma DNA in Startup Land

Brahma, in Sanskrit ब्रह्मा, *is a Hindu God referred to as 'the Creator'. He is associated with creation, knowledge, and the Vedas.*

In Bharat's land of unicorns and upcoming
brands,
Where Brahma's spirit sweeps across the lands,
A cosmic dance of growth unfolds,
As founders' dreams turn into gold.
Employees, heed the Brahma way,
Growth and focus are founders' DNA.
Multitasking has become second nature,

Four-dimensional thinking is now a key feature.
With four heads spinning, all thinking ideas galore,
Nothing is off-limits, open to explore,
His first face sees the future bright,
The second codes through day and night,
The third face handles HR with care,
The fourth keeps finances fair and square.
From zero to one, then one to many,
Brahma—The founder does all roles, not missing any.

Corporate Annual Utsava

Utsava, in Sanskrit उत्सव, *means 'a festival or celebration'.*

One leader calls it, "Synergy Summit?" Too
cliché!
Another one suggests, "Innovation Ignite?"
Passé!
"Samavesh," suggests someone in ranks low,
It is Sanskrit for 'inclusion', perhaps few may
know.
Thumbs up emoji on corporate WhatsApp
comes up lightning fast,
As they have found the perfect name for the
annual day, at last.
The cafeteria is now a grand pandal,
Serves vada pav and pasta; how global!

Potluck diversity on eco-friendly plates,
A culinary UN of all the Indian states.
Rangoli in the lobby, made of exotic flowers and notes,
Post-its arranged with colorful quotes.
The talent show, a corporate Ram Leela,
Where the shy coder becomes Sita.
And quiet admin takes the stage,
As a stand-up comic, and all laugh in rage!
All in festive harmony, prove that beyond targets and bottom lines,
The spirit of corporate utsava truly shines!

Chandra Cycles

*Chandra, in Sanskrit चन्द्र, is the Hindu Moon
God associated with the night, plants, and
vegetation.*

Like the moon that waxes and wanes,
Her moods ebb and flow with hormonal refrains.
One day, she's bright as the full moon's gleam,
Next, she's crescent-shaped, it would seem.
Her colleagues whisper, "Is it that time again?"
As if her competence is tied to a lunar vein.
Managers scratch heads at her changing tide,
Not realizing the strength it takes to ride.
The waves of pain, bloating, and fatigue,
While still crushing deadlines despite weakened
physique.
Remember men, and women too,
During the Chandra cycle, showing empathy is
the best thing to do.

Vipassana – Mindful Leadership

Vipassana *means 'to see things as they really are'.*

Vipassana is the buzz, the corporate craze,
Transforming leaders in surprising ways.
No more power lunches or golf course deals,
It's all about how the breath feels.
Morality, focus, and wisdom combined,
Creating leaders of a different kind.
Dharma's universal laws they learn,
While quarterly profits, they need to earn.
But now they seek a different wealth,
Inner peace, balance, and mental health.
In silence they sit, hour after hour,

Discovering a new kind of power.
No emails, no calls, no PowerPoint,
Just breathing in and out, and that's the point.
Mindfulness metrics are now on the company chart,
KPIs now include an open heart.
Vipassana-trained leaders are now making the corporate climb,
Feeling joy, one breath at a time!

Draupadi and Sita – Women Leaders

Draupadi in the epic Mahabharata was noted for her beauty and courage. *Sita*, in the epic Ramayana, was noted for her beauty and devotion. Both were the leading female protagonists of these two epics.

In two of the most important Indian epics old, two tales unfold,
Of women strong, both their stories are bold.
For Sita, quiet strength was her game,
In integrity tests, she'd put others to shame.
Her emotional intelligence was off the charts,
In team building, she'd win all the parts.
Strategic thinking was Draupadi's secret weapon,
In corporate chess, she'd be a grandmaster, there's no question!

Adaptability? Both wrote the book!
From palace to forest, whatever it took.
Decision-making was firm, with grace under
fire,
In change management, both never tire.
So, lean in, ladies, with these legends as your
guide,
In the corporate Kurukshetra, women leaders
turn the tide.
With Draupadi's fire and Sita's quiet power,
Watch women's leadership skills begin to
flower!

Balancing Act

Here's to the dad who rocks the suit,
And the mom who manages the budget astute.
To the stay-at-home spouse, a domestic pro,
Whose management skills make households
grow.
Whether they conquer markets or clear
mountains of toys,
Lead meetings or share parenting joys,
Here's to a world where all roles shine,
Inclusive culture, like a family including yours
and mine.
May we judge not by gender but win by heart,
Create a balanced workforce where LGBTQs
play a part.
For in homes and offices, the truth is bare,
It's not about gender, but the common purpose
we share.

Crowning Glory: Return to Work

The post-pandemic exile, it seems, must end,
Though many remote workers will surely
contend.
Coming back from great resignation; upgrade
from pajamas to suits,
As they trade in comfy slippers for work boots.
Newton's First Law now put to the test,
As tech companies put the work from home to
rest.
They're luring with goodies and snacks, and
perks galore,
To show up in person with the promise of much
more.
But lurking behind, a pink slip threat looms,

For those who prefer their own home-office
rooms.
It's like Rama's return to Ayodhya, they say,
But we're not quite sure who Sita is in this play.
Is it the employee, crowned with office swag?
Or the investors, whose profits started to sag?
As the world returns from pandemic
self-imposed exiles,
Let's hope it's worth all the gas and the miles.

Me Too

In times of kingdoms and palaces, a tale as old
as time,
Men of might and corrupt power, like
Duryodhana, committed a heinous crime.
Dragging Draupadi in the hall,
Stripped of dignity and made her fall,
Fast Forward to the 21st century, the dice of fate
have turned,
As women's voices, long unheard.
"Me Too!" they cried, a chorus so strong,
Exposing wrong deeds swept under for too long.
They stood up tall, their stories told,
A movement was born—brave and bold.
Corporate now brings a ray of hope,
They call it the POSH Act, helping impacted
women cope.
Prevention, prohibition, and redressal too,
A legal shield that was long overdue.
For every Draupadi they've wronged,

A thousand voices grew strong.
The work culture is changing with rules anew,
Respect and consent, long overdue.
So, here's to POSH, to #MeToo's might,
To women standing up for what is fair and right.

C-Suite Gurus

Guru, in Sanskrit गुरु, *means mentor, guide, expert, or master of certain knowledge or field.*

Six archetypes from mythology, we wish to see
on the corporate stage.
Like **Gurus** of old, these leaders can shape our
fate,
With lessons learned, some small and some
great.
Dronacharya, the CEO with a moonshot dream,
With skills so sharp and intellect supreme.
Vishwamitra, the CFO, with investor pressures
he won't give in,
His perseverance, sure to help him and his CEO
win.
Vashistha, the mindfulness CHRO and coach,
Teaching stressed execs to follow a Zen
approach.
Valmiki, the CMO, who can pen the corporate
Ramayana,

With great PR skills, crafting compelling stories
with viral drama.
Ved Vyas, the CDO to the very core,
Making sense of data as the guru of the ancient
lore.
Agastya, the CEO advisor, turning disruptive
ideas into gold,
Sniffing wins from lost deals with potential
manifolds.

50/Fifty

In corporate boardrooms where wisdom and courage convene,
Women leaders over fifty are still few and far between,
The ones who made it are role models with powerful voices clear,
Shaping the future of theirs and others without fear.
For these leaders are climbing the ladder on a global stage,
And writing new chapters in their age.
From financial independence to true freedom is their sweet song,
They are paving the way, proving their naysayers wrong.

Shaping companies, economies, and more,
They are the driving force we cannot ignore.
Resilience and mental strength—they are
figuring it all,
With emotional quotient, they stand tall.
But let's not forget our male allies too,
We need their unwavering support to see us
through.
A tribute to their strength of triumph, worthy of
praise,
Women leaders, be ready to lead and pay it
forward with grace.